The One That God Built

A Book of Poems

Steve Johnson

WESTBOW
PRESS®
A DIVISION OF THOMAS NELSON
& ZONDERVAN

Scripture quotations taken from the New American Standard Bible® (NASB),
Copyright © 1960, 1962, 1963, 1968, 1971, 1972, 1973,
1975, 1977, 1995 by The Lockman Foundation
Used by permission. www.Lockman.org

Photos are by Shonda Judy of Cynthiana, Kentucky

Edited by Lori Rawlins

WestBow Press books may be ordered through booksellers or by contacting:

WestBow Press
A Division of Thomas Nelson & Zondervan
1663 Liberty Drive
Bloomington, IN 47403
www.westbowpress.com
1 (866) 928-1240

ISBN: 978-1-5127-6707-0 (sc)
ISBN: 978-1-5127-6708-7 (e)

Library of Congress Control Number: 2016920503

Print information available on the last page.

WestBow Press rev. date: 12/9/2016

CONTENTS

ACKNOWLEDGEMENTS AND CREDITS

The poems in this collection are spontaneous writings that reflect the thoughts or visions I had after I had been blessed with a moment of wonder. Many are of encouragement; others are from pure awe after meeting or observing someone while they were unaware of my presence.

I would like to thank Lori Rawlins, Kathy Rose, Shonda Judy, my wife Karen, my family and many others who have ventured in and out of my life. They each in their own way provided me with an emotional moment that would not fade till I put it on paper.

DANIEL'S CRY

Oh my King Darius, my heart has become so
    distressed.
You signed this decree; I can't accept your request.
    You are my King but My God comes first.
    He gives me my bread and quenches my thirst.

This is not my home; it's through this window to the
    west.
To my living God I give thanks for this test.
I know I'll be caught giving all glory to my Lord.
He speaks truth with a tongue like a double-edged
    sword.

His commandments are more than simple requests.
He won't accept "I did my best!"
He controls all Earthly power, so to Him I must kneel.
Nothing I do can alter his will.

My Lord can deliver me, or he can stand by my side.
Whatever he chooses is not for me to decide.
He can feed the lions; they belong to Him too.
I have no say in what he wants to do.

In this lion's den, sealed tight with a stone.
Anxiety engulfs me as I sit all alone.

The darkness surrounds me as a wet fog full of gloom.
Knowing my Lord is with me, I accept my doom.

The lions show no emotion, not one of them care.
Their mouths shut by an angel; they just lie there and
  stare.
Not knowing God's plan. I patiently wait in the night
To see what he gives me when this dark turns to light.

I hear King Darius as he hurries to see.
If My God delivered me, He can set me free.
I have been spared by a God wise and so clever.
Come see, King Darius. Oh, King, live forever.

Life vs. Time

As life moves on, we absorb the cost
Of things left unsaid or time we have lost.
Time we can't destroy, nor can we create.
So engulf each moment; don't consider it just fate.
Observe those around you; they all have their needs.
They mostly need love or compassion, not your deeds

Sounds of Peace

As we travel along under cloudy skies.
A light mist falls as our spirit cries.
Searching ever for things we can't see.
We reach to our Lord with a yearning plea.

We all need to search, but we must listen to hear.
Take time to calm down; this world do not fear.
It's those times when we hear nothing at all
He says the most, sends out His call.

When you have been chosen, paid for with blood,
Let Him choose your path, although it's through mud.
Turn off the noises, the chatter from your mind.
From Him you'll get peace; His rest you'll find.

Happy Mother's Day

We've set aside this special day to recognize all
    mothers.
For they're the ones who cared for us, displayed love
    above all others.
Give your respect to all the ladies so they know that
    they are special.
They made you who you are; for that you should be
    grateful.

Beyond Closed Doors

Life was closing in as if I were choked.
Raining on my soul, my spirit was soaked.
Hours after midnight, no sight of dawn.
Sitting in a vacuum, all options were gone.
I pondered how I got here, what I'd lost along the way.
Knowing I was lost, it must be time to pray.
I searched throughout my fortress for a door to set me
    free.
But if I found a door, who might have the key?
I heard someone knocking; I hurried to find the spot.
Now I was in a panic; my stomach in a knot.
Not knowing what to do, I paused for just awhile,
And standing next to me was Jesus with a smile
"Did I do wrong?" I asked. I don't understand or see.
"It's okay now," He replied. "You forgot to wait for me."
So He tore down my fortress, cleaned up my trash and
    guilt.
Set me on my knees, and let my anguish wilt.
He turned and spoke to me when He finished with His
    chores.
Be careful whom you leave behind when you're closing
    the door.

Who is your provider

If you would take time out to watch God's creatures of
   life.
See how they survive without self-created strife.
They take life's chores, the things that must be done.
Simplify their tasks, make them appear as almost fun.
They take what God hands them for it's only his to give.
Accept it and use it, but only what's required to live.
Letting God have His glory, "Why?" they never ask.
Doing only what's required, adding nothing to their task.
Once they've served their purpose, they move on or
   drift away.
But He decides their futures or what they need
   each day.
Yet we continue to worry and try to achieve much more.
You need only to consider Luke 12:24.

Pictures: Shonda Judy

7

CICADAS

Ever wonder why cicadas come every seventeen
  years?
Or why God turned them loose to stir up our fears?
They have destructive appetites and a loud,
  screeching buzz.
But He has specific reasons for all that He does.
Like all His other mysteries that drift in my mind.
The answers aren't clear and many hard to find.
For now I'll be patient. He'll tell me in time.
But maybe He won't; it's His choice, not mine.

Morning Meditation

Hard to grasp the peace that comes in the morning
chill.
Waiting on the sun, yet all remains still.
Like staring in a springtime puddle, nothing there
to see.
An empty, clear reflection that soon will not be.
I think of those around me, and the new friends I've
made.
As the joy swells inside me; the chill begins to fade.
So glad my Lord has blessed me with all I need.
Many times just what I want, my spirit He'll always
feed.
Shake off the old, start this day all new.
The past is done, let bad memories be few.
You always have hope, no need to despair.
Pay attention and discover the ones who really care.

Hiding in the Dark

A homeless man lies soaking up the dew.
I convince myself there is nothing "I" can do.
So I change my path as I stroll through the park.
But you know what? I'm just hiding in the dark.

A sister is hurting; her broken heart cries.
So I drop my head and don't look in her eyes.
Just walk on by acting happy as a lark.
But you know what? I'm just hiding in the dark.

Children are neglected all over the land.
They are asking for anyone to lend a hand.
I say, "I can help." But I'm all bark.
'Cause you know why? I'm just hiding in the dark.

A stranger is stranded; his car won't run.
Can't stop now; this is my day for fun.
Besides that, there is no place to park.
But you know what? I'm just hiding in the dark.

I walk into church and look for the last pew.
Don't go any further, this spot will do.
I'll just lie low, so I won't leave my mark.
But you know what? I'm just hiding in the dark.

So if you go ask God what you can do.
Be prepared; He'll probably tell you
Be like Noah, penned up in the ark,
Open a window and quit hiding in the dark.

THINGS TO COME

The beauty and joy that follow a new moment,
The blessings of peace, all things God sent.
I pray for those who only see with the eye
For beyond their vision, the important things lie.
In the peace of the moment, a wisp of clouds drift by,
Like the passing of thoughts from my mind's outcry.
Just clusters of memories filtered by dreams,
Leaving melancholy feelings: not all's as it seems.
So I start this day with hope all is true.
Clear out my mind and start all things new.

SOLITARY

Can anyone hear a weary heart's plea?
When you stand strong, can no one see?
Life slips away, as holding onto loose sand.
You have to endure, though alone you stand.
Always in a dark space, no doors are found.
Engulfed by emptiness, no light or sound.
What is on this Earth offers no true prize.
What really matters is in our Father's eyes.

RECIPE

Each jar of jam is unique in its own way,
Though it was made the same time, same day.
Now this one is sweeter, and this one is kinda runny.
Here's one that's grainy, and this one tastes funny.
But when you take just one jar all alone,
Savor the flavor, none like you've known.
You never notice the flaws that are there
When there is nothing around for you to compare.
Now God made us all with His own recipe,
But I'll tell you now: you're nothing like me.
You'll understand if you take time to reflect.
Nothing on Earth is ever perfect.

Picture: Shonda Judy

THE BOOK

I was in this room just barely lit, emptiness all around,
resting all alone.
Leaning back, I opened up my soul to let my spirit out
to roam.
As it drifted off toward endless space, it lost all shape
or form,
Like fog on a frosty morning from a hillside pond still
warm.
There was something else in there with me, its
presence persistent to be found.
But nothing could I hear, nothing could I smell, nothing
could I see, though I searched all around.
So I thought I would continue with my journey. That's
when I saw "the book."
A piece of work from a special friend, so I thought I'd
take a look.
I thought about what it represented, whom it was
from, there came a smile upon my face.
And once again I could feel I wasn't alone inside my
space.
I sat in my mystery, my eyes focused on its cover as I
lifted it from my side.
I placed my hand on the cover, stroked across the
front, and thought of what's inside.

When I stroked across the cover, an affectionate
gesture from me, I received the most tender
surprise.
An emotional rush from my groin up through my
chest, and tears came to my eyes.
Then the warmth spread throughout me, from my feet
up through my hand.
Then a spirit spoke softly to me, and I began to
understand.
No longer aware of my Earthly surroundings, I tried
intently to hear.
All my senses were awakened, and yet I had no fear.
I felt only comfort and joy, a happiness most never feel
As the spirit settled in, the character it began to
reveal.
I was allowed to see the heart, how it has been so true
and pure.
A special one in this universe, of this I was sure.
Our spirits bonded forever; what this means, who will
ever know?
But like all friends, they are with me, always, where
ever I go.
My life is different now, a better person I'll be,
Because in one brief moment, they became part of me.

The Herdsman's Revenge

(Taking care of the flock)

I will care for the herd; it's always in need.
I'll scatter the hay and prepare the feed
So they can come at their own free will,
To feast on the feed, till they've had their fill.

Most of them stand back with a watchful eye,
Waiting for me to finish, I guess they're just shy.
When I start to leave, they come up to feast.
They pay me no mind now, to say the least.

Some of the others respond in greed.
They come rushing up to take what they need.
No matter what they've already had,
The way they respond, you'd think they were mad.

They trample my feet and knock me around.
It's all I can do to not be knocked down.
If I don't survive, doesn't matter to them.
They're confident someone will show up again.

There is one more group; their numbers are small.

They're sneaky and cruel and dislike us all.
They hide behind me and stay out of sight,
Then charge after me when the time is right.

Why I am there is not their concern.
They don't care if I ever return.
Why they dislike me, there is no excuse.
Their whole life is a pattern of hate and abuse.

But tomorrow when I go to the field,
If I find one in peril, looks like its fate has been sealed.
I'll do what it takes to set it free,
Knowing tomorrow it will come right back at me.

Although I watch over them and provide them care,
In the back of my mind I'm always aware.
Each one is different; even they don't know why
They do what they do or try what they try.

I will watch over them at the Master's request.
Continue on and do my best.
Till the day He comes to tell me when
Cull out the wicked ones
FOR THE SLAUGHTERHOUSE PEN!

WHAT IS PRECIOUS

Soaking up the sunshine, sitting all alone,
Ah, feeling his spirit, knowing that you're God's own.
See the brilliant colors; made just for you and me.
Look beyond your vision, there's more that you
    can see.
Everything around you, created by His hands.
Knowing in solemn peace, with you, He forever stands.
Your life may seem in shambles, a mystery, nothing's
    real.
But all is as it should be, God just acting out His will.

"Ol' John"

It has four rubber tires,
Kind of long and lean.
If it's my tractor,
It's painted John Deere green.

Untouched by time,
Although it's fifty years old.
It still pulls with the passion
Of a miner after gold.

When the day's work is done,
Daylight is drifting away;
I'll put it in the shed.
Ol' John's done for the day.
As I wipe off the dust,
Silence drifts all around,
Ol' John grunts and sighs
As his motor cools down.

THE SERVANT

Sometimes we wonder who we are.
It often seems someone afar.
And you wonder, "What do they think of me?'
'Cause you really are what others see.

You took God's gift He made just for you.
It's yours alone, no matter what you do.
Can't give it to the kids or share it with your wife;
It's yours now for the rest of your life.

You choose to serve and share your life
For those of us who live in strife.
Although I'm grateful, it does not matter,
The important thing is keep climbing God's ladder.

Fourth of July

God gave us this country, made free and bold.
Today is her birthday over 200 years old.
The privileges we share compare to no other.
By the blood left behind of a sister or brother.
We must remain ready to answer the call,
Or over time we will watch her fall.
Lord, please cover us with wisdom and valor.
Save our country, help us stand up taller.
Let us remember those who never asked why
As we celebrate this 4th of July.

FRIENDS

WHO ARE THEY

The mystery of one's essence is easily obscured.
For those of special quality at times not seen or heard.
They bring with them a presence only few are aware.
Like a fog consumes the space, unnoticed like the air.
Those who are conscious can feel their very worth,
And are truly thankful they reside here on Earth.
Their presence lifts you up and brings joy when you
     are down.
By sharing all they are, a greater gift cannot be found.
These ladies are often forgotten, at times
     misunderstood,
Seldom get a thank you, or reward for all their good.
So I take this time to highlight them and give them
     their due.
To shine a bright spot on them, for they are the few.

Inspired by Kathy

BIRTHDAY WISHES

Giving some thought to this special day.
I wonder why God did things this way.
He sent a gift here this day on Earth.
A beautiful spirit became human by birth.
Your presence is a pleasure.
Your worth beyond measure.
Your smile is your light; your own hidden treasure

Inspired by Kathy

The Silent Friend

Looking back to years past, to those you've been
  around.
If you examine these encounters, sometimes a friend is
  found.
We fail to even notice them as we focus on our task.
Don't ever note their presence, as hidden behind a
  mask.
If you listen to their silence, be patient and you will
  hear,
The sound of their compassion, whether far or near.
Though not always obvious, in their quietness they
  blend.
These are the special ones I call "The Silent Friend."

They seem always to be occupied, and seldom show
  emotion.
When they speak it's short and simple, with words
  carefully chosen.
There is no need for flattery; they know just who
  they are.
Hidden among the scenery, a dull glow from afar.
Not always eager to respond, doesn't mean that they
  don't care.
But knowing you can count on them is the bond you
  truly share.

No empty words to lift you up or advice they
   recommend.
It's not that they don't feel your need; they are "The
   Silent Friend."

Born of the highest character, they too still have their
   needs.
So return to them your clemency, don't offer them
   your deeds.
Remember those that feel the most don't always stand
   so tough.
It's them at times that need the most; they've often
   had enough.
The light emitted from their eyes, a smile so faint yet
   bold,
Hold the clues from their heart; the story yet untold.
Though invisible to the eyes, all others they transcend
These are the special ones I call "The Silent Friend."

Inspired by Kathy

On this special day, a miracle performed.
A father's smile, a mother's heart warmed.
The Lord reached out, took a star from the sky,
Gave it your soul, put its light in your eye.
An enigma in your silence, a presence to know,
Not quite clinquant, but as a soft warm glow.
Our thoughts of you are sent your way
Take a moment and smile, IT'S YOUR BIRTHDAY!

Inspired by Kathy

A Christmas Note

As you taste your morning coffee,
and tabulate this fervid day,
Across the field toward the morning sun,
We too have chores set on their way.
We wish you joy above all emotions,
Cherished memories for this season.
A Savior was born for us this day,
Why He chose us there is no reason.

BEAUTY VS. TIME

The feelings that come to life and leave my soul in
wonder,
When a special moment presents itself, on real life I do
ponder.
Then God revealed to me, the beauty of His making.
Nothing that my eyes could see, inside my heart was
aching.
I saw two ladies strolling by, no particular destination.
Then I was presented with a vision, a reverie invasion.

These ladies delivered babies and raised their
children up.
Passed out love, played the nurse, shed tears to fill
a cup.
The anxiety built up within them, with their hearts full
of fear.
They watched their children leave, each one a
different year.
Now they're back to watching little ones, a generation
apart.
I wonder how they keep it up, how did it ever start?

They have worked for the public for more than twenty
years.

A daily dose of stress they get, unwanted noise in the
ears.
They give attention to their parents of the most loving
kind;
So many times they get rejected, resentment's all they
find.
With all that they have in their lives, they have a
husband too.
As he wanders in and out each day, he doesn't have a
clue.

These thoughts roam in my mind, as the wind blows
through their hair.
Their forms barely come in focus through the sun's
blasting glare.
I watch them walk throughout the stones in the
fashion of a child.
No real expression on their face, their manner light
and mild.
Without a word they turn to leave, to their own world
return.
For me it's just a memory to make my insides burn.

The turmoil they've had in their past, I can hardly tell.
In a graceful motion, they float by, as if all is well.
True beauty in this life will set your soul on fire.
These moments I have here on Earth are all that I desire.
This vision God has blessed me with, who knows what
it means?
These ladies survived all life dealt to them and still
look good in jeans!

Inspired by Karen & Kathy

Angel of the Moment

Lost in a fog, no sense of time,
I gently took a seat.
Withdrawn deep inside myself,
The future seemed so bleak.
I must have been invisible,
My presence was ignored.
I only wished my usual self,
Could somehow be restored.
So I sat there tired, in a daze,
All alone in my torment.
Yet, you, with crystal eyes, a simple smile,
Became my angel for the moment.

Inspired by Geri

PORTRAIT OF A FRIEND

When the Master of the universe made the choice for
who you are;
He looked through the Galaxy and chose the brightest
star.
The inspiration you are to others, a light to draw them
near.
To stir their minds, make them dream, and grasp for
something dear.
You'll probably never know the peace and joy you
bring,
As in a park listening, to a distant church bell ring.
In the blessing of your presence, one always seems to
find,
A spirit soft, a heart so young, an active, gifted mind.
Nothing seems to stir the heart as when your thoughts
you share,
And listen to what others say, then your thoughts
compare.
Your beauty lies within you, the sum of all you are.
Not always obvious or visible, but as a welcomed glow
afar.
We know not what lives we'll touch or what roads we'll
travel down;
New ones that we chance to meet or old ones not
around

So cherish all your talents, grasp each moment of
 everyday.
Give all the chance to know you, and put a bright spot
 in their day.
Don't worry about the past, or things you can't undo.
There's nothing to forgive, for those who know you.
A diamond, sure and pure, set in a band of gold.
Why God made you like you are, is a mystery still
 untold.
If a day should ever come, you're feeling all alone,
We're waiting with a ray of light, that on us you have
 shone.
For those who strike against you, they'll understand in
 the end,
You're really not a threat to them, only just a friend.

The greatest friend

THE SPIRIT OF A SPECIAL ONE

The spirit of a special one drifts throughout the room.
Brings bursts of joy and gladness, to chase out
    unwanted gloom.
Like the bubbles from a champagne glass, all
    bitterness released.
The euphoria inside you is lifted up and unleashed.
All of this accomplished, by such a special one.
A blessing to be around, to share in all the fun.
A heart of a child that has not yet been defiled.
One so full of laughter, by her, you won't be reviled.
Always with an answer, quite witty sometimes bold.
A teacher to the little ones, inspiration for the old.
Always full of energy, a presence so indelible.
Confident and caring, all said she's quite incredible.

Inspired by Lori

All kinds of people live in this land,
But the ones like you will lend a hand.
To stand up and do your part,
And give a gift that's from the heart.
The uniform you gave,
Will do someone well.
SO REMEMBER
Compassion and kindness are not for sale.

Inspired by Kaylee

Here's your blog, it's day two,
Still cold outside, more soup for you.
I kind of like it all brisk and clear,
Steam off the cattle as distant sounds tickle the ear,
So-o-o take a big stretch, put a big smile on your face,
Sit back and enjoy what God's put in place.

Inspired by Shonda

JERRY

Always a laugh, with a spirit so kind,
Influenced by no one, he was self-refined.
Full of life's passion, a heart on fire,
A good sporting battle was his greatest desire.
A pocket full of pranks, yea - Mr. Cool.
Try turning the tables? Nah, he's nobody's fool!
To some he was Grand Pa, to others he was Dad,
Who could forget the pictures he had?
 His future was full, so well planned,
Then, a turn of events we can't understand.
Like a raging wave as it crashes to land,
It changes the shoreline and removes the sand.
He made his plans like we all do,
But God came and took him; he had bigger things
    to do.
Down here his spirit was restricted and bound;
Up there he's free to travel around.
So instead of caring for only family or friend,
He can watch over the world from end to end

To those who follow : The descendants of Jerry Paul Mitcheltree

HEIRLOOM

As the holidays get closer and my mind starts to
    ponder,
I think of you and my thoughts start to wander.
Like a precious heirloom, lost in some space,
You were not forgotten, just been misplaced.
A soft spirit that faded away in the night,
Not sure where you were –for sure out of sight.
Now you've appeared all shiny like new,
But to my delight, it was the same old you.
I hope you will stay, no need for an end.
From past years till now, you're my special friend.

IDENTITY

When your world drifts off as a distant star,
You start to wonder who you are.
It's all out of reach, just a big black hole.
Nothing makes sense, no food for your soul.
So you reach to the world for something secure,
But to your disappointment, you find nothing's for
    sure.
It is in this world our troubles evolved.
Yet beyond this world, they can be solved.
It doesn't matter what others do,
Our Lord and Savior knows just who's who.
Through His love you're always the same.
You are so special, just what is your name?
So when you are down, and you feel so dumb,
            REMEMBER!
The world can't take away who you've become!

Inspired by Shirley

Danny & Shonda

Today my mind drifts back twenty years,
I walk down the aisle full of anxiety and fears.
Mom, Dad, the children, the violin, all my friends,
The Messenger's Quartet, and my sister, the list never
    ends.
The maids standing with me dressed in satin of black.
The ring bearer approaches and never looks back.
The rings are tied neatly to a little Steiff bear,
A gift from Danny full of love and care.
The ceremony starts with Uncle Emmitt in prayer,
The benediction by Wayne Smith, he, too, was there.
Dad does the ceremony, trying to hold back his tears.
We light the unity candle, our oneness appears.
We say our vows; the future's ours to seek.
Then I see a tear sliding down Danny's cheek.
A long line of hugs, then the reception,
All Nana's food, there were no exceptions.
Danny takes the garter, I feel everyone stare.
I toss the bouquet up high without care.
The birdseed was tossed, the balloons set free,
The limo ride; it was all for me.
At a bed and breakfast in Versailles, it all came to end;
From this moment forward a new life begins.
Two lives together turn out to be one.
What God has joined shall not be undone.

He took two imperfect people, blended them just right.
Now there are two special children, a perfect delight.
Twenty years ago a best friend was met
As the sun goes down, together we sit.

Rare Encounters

Yesterday
I was blessed with conversation, not really much to
   mention.
A lady not afraid to speak, had no agenda, no
   intention.
Just simple words put together to express a simple
   thought.
Not passing judgment or accusations, just the truth
   was sought.
These encounters seem rare these days, yet they are
   there to find.
They are not for us to analyze, just food for our mind.

Inspired by Melissa

NEW LOVE

Yesterday I met a man of four score years,
Who spoke of a new love as he fought back tears.
A God-fearing man, yet he was about to wilt,
Because of friends who plagued him with guilt.
Why do we judge others, tear them apart,
With ideas of the mind and not joy from the heart?

Inspired by Billy

I Am

When life is a mystery, you wonder who you are;
Everything is out of reach, a distance too far.
Not sure where you are, but you can see where you've
     been,
You've been chasing a circle you know has no end.
Remember you're special, there's no one like you,
And you have the power to make your dreams come
     true.
The Lord didn't make you because He had nothing
     to do;
He planned it all out and made you brand new.
There is someone inside you trying to get out,
To show the world around you what you're all about.
The world will tell you, you have no purpose on Earth.
If you decide to stand up, they will see what you're
     worth.
I'm glad that I know you, and one day you'll see;
Your decisions made today decide who you will be.

FAMILY

Madi's Christmas

Another year has drifted by,
Now you say you're five,
The baby Jesus' birthday comes,
His spirit's still alive,
We celebrate his birthday,
And call it Christmas Day.
I think about a year ago,
You were quite well on your way.
You've changed so much we can't keep up,
I can almost see you grow.
It seems you've also learned a lot,
"GIGI, I told you so."
Off to school, throw rocks in the creek,
OOPS! There's mud on your pants.
Kick your shoe clear off the stage,
When you do your dance.
So is it any wonder,
With excitement I almost cry,
When I think of next year,
Who knows? You'll probably fly!

Bryce

How could a bundle so tiny and small;
Make your insides so weak you just might fall?
Such a short time you've been in my life.
I pray for your happiness; a life without strife.
I hope your first Christmas brings you much cheer,
And I'll learn all about you throughout the next year.
You've started to smile, your eyes are now clear,
When Mommy's too slow they turn loose a tear.
Talking to Daddy late at night,
Won't take too long before you say it just right.
I have no control of what lies ahead,
So for now I'll have to hold and love you instead.

PERRAUTS

The Christmas season is almost here,
So I take some time to spread some cheer.
The two of you have brought me so much joy.
You brought home a girl, then a boy.
The four of you seem to blend so well,
I'm sure you're not perfect but who could tell.
God has blessed you in so many ways,
You spread warmth all around as the sun's rays.
I pray for your happiness, peace for your mind,
Love for each other, and all the joy you can find.
God only knows what plans lie ahead,
There's nothing to say that hasn't been said.
I love you each one, that's why I'm here,
To guard, protect, and calm your fear.

JASON

It's almost Christmas, the end of the year.
A time of peace, hope, love and cheer.
When I look at what you've achieved.
I feel so proud all worries relieved.
We used to knock heads; you had so much to say.
But I couldn't hear, no time that day.
You had places to go, respect to earn,
All said and done, I had the most to learn.
God blessed you as though he cast a spell.
Like your grandpa, you read people well.
For your peace, love and joy I pray every day.
But in the end it's not for me to say.
All these things are for you to take,
Blessings come from the choices we make.
No matter what road you choose to roam;
There's always a place to rest here at home.

WEDDING

Take imperfect elements,
Blend them just right,
A new object created,
A perfect delight!
It takes patience and care,
To produce a fine wine,
Now God made you one,
No more yours or mine.
Let love fill your hearts,
Time fill your soul,
Age make you wiser,
And God make you whole.

MADISON

Little Madison has a big beautiful smile,
With brown-green eyes you can see for a mile.
She'll run and hide when you come around,
Stay there and giggle until she is found.
"Wanna play outside?" she asks when Daddy comes
    home,
and all through the yard she'll stumble and roam.
Giovanni's where Nana takes her for lunch,
Bring me the cinnamon sticks, a whole big bunch.
Madison,
You fill up my heart with happiness and such,
I can't wait till Christmas I love you so much.

New Beginning

When a new seed is planted,
In God's wisdom it must die.
Before a new sprout evolves,
Then it looks to the sky.
So you take your past,
And bury it deep.
Today you make promises,
Each other you'll keep.
Cherish time you're together,
Let your souls intertwine.
May God give you insight,
All else will be fine.

For Jason & Lindsay

Reflections

"18"

From a little girl with giggles and laughs,
Now almost grown, with a touch of class.
From tinseled teeth and short bobbed hair,
To a bright young lady so cheery and fair.
A special young lady we've always been proud,
Except when you "BURP" way too loud!
To the joy you have brought us, there is no measure,
Being around you is an absolute pleasure.
The past eighteen years, they're gone, like an autumn
   breeze,
But our memories stand still, and our hearts are
   pleased.

We love you
"HAPPY BIRTHDAY"

REBECCA JOHNSON

October 26, 1982

WIFE

Karen

BIRTHDAY WISHES

I wonder how the stars aligned,
When the Lord brought you to Earth.
I didn't know who you were,
Didn't celebrate your birth.
Our paths crossed in time,
Two souls became one.
Still quite a mystery,
Just what we had begun.
For sure, in all His might,
The Lord performed His best,
To create you just for me,
My life forever blessed.
HAPPY BIRTHDAY!

Where would I be if this day never was?
What would I do if I didn't have a cause?
You wouldn't be here to stand by my side;
I would have no one to be my guide.
But, as it is you came on nine May,
I give thanks to the Lord it is your birthday.

ANNIVERSARY

Seems it was from another life,
Back in "75" she became my wife.
A lot has transpired in these 39 years.
Two kids, three grandkids and a few tears.
We'll remain together no matter where;
We understand how much we each care.
Joined together, a gift from above,
One more year to share our love.

OUR TIME

In 2015 our time counted, an even twenty plus a score;
So many emotions from the memories we store.
No matter how we got here the past we can't change;
Yet look at the future and the world appears strange.
We exist in the present; this is the moment to live;
If you come with me, we'll find more to give.
My every thought evolves with you on my mind;
When the world interferes, only emptiness I find.
 I offer to you all the love we can share;
Come walk with me, make one from a pair.

VALENTINE

Again I consider how far we've come,
Thirty-five years not as long as some.
We think so different, your thoughts, I can't tell;
But all in all don't we go together well?
I like to move; you like to sit still.
No common place, this can't be real.
So much to do, places we could roam,
But, at the end of the day, we both come home.
God picked you out; this one's for you.
When I saw you, what else could I do?
But ask you to join me, walk the same line;
Now on this special day, be my Valentine.

February 14th two thousand nine,
Time to ask, "Be my valentine?"
Always in a rush, constantly on the go,
Who is that guy? I don't know.
I'm the guy that loves you so.
Dear Valentine, will you be mine?

CHRISTMAS THIRTY-TWO

Here we are at Christmas thirty-two,
A perfect time to share a thought of you.
I think about the history we've made,
And our younger years that have started to fade.
There were trips to town to grind the feed,
To pick up supplies that we might need,
Stop at the Dairybarn for two chilidogs,
Hurry home to feed the hogs.

We had just settled in when Jason arrived,
Iced and snowed in, we barely survived.
Dirty diapers in the stripping room, what a mess!
Times like these, we were at our best.
He won't go to sleep, wants to stay up late,
Pen him in, and he sleeps on the gate.
Rush to the hospital to put in some stitches,
He bites the nurse against all our wishes.

Take a deep breath because Rebecca dropped in,
No sleep, and fixin' bottles all over again.
Between college and farming we just want to sob,
Pack up, we're moving, Daddy's got a job.
Send her to school, and now Mommy's employed.
Remember the pig, everyone enjoyed?

She's draggin' home friends, don't remember their
   names,
Load up the car, for the football games.

Jason's gone now; Rebecca got married,
And we've forgotten the load we once carried.
Driving to Richmond, awaiting the time
I can give it all up, and each day will be mine.
Time has gone by so fast it's hard to remember
All the special moments, and now it's December.
By the time we learned that we weren't insane,
Look out! Two grandbabies! Here we go again!

We've floated apart as barges adrift,
It's time for some changes; we need to downshift.
You're so very special; there is no one like you,
That's why I chose you, who else would do?
Sometimes I see that you don't understand,
Just how it feels when you touch my hand.
So don't sell yourself short, you've been blessed from
   above;
Sit back and relax so you can feel the love.

The roses aren't red,
The envelope's not blue,
And you probably don't know,
How much I love you.
Sometimes we're so distant,
It's long overdue,
When we think of each other,

All the day through.
So tomorrow's a new day,
Fresh and brand new,
So let's be one,
And put away the two.

One Special Day

The last few months have been filled with strife.
Now, this is the first day of the rest of "our" life.
Together we must go on,
To see what awaits the dawn,
I still need you to be my wife.

In seventy-five we were brand new,
Twenty-seven years later we're back to two.
The kids were fun,
But we're not really done,
Let's make this our time, it's way overdue.

The definitions for love are many;
The value of talk is less than a penny.
If we only would start
Each day from the heart,
Our blessings together would be more than plenty.

God searches our hearts for love that is true;
Mine was empty so He sent you.
Our time he has blessed,
Each day's a new best,
It's all about Him, and we've much to do.

ANNIVERSARY

From my youngest days till the time we met,
My journey through life has always been set.
All the desires that never came to be;
The things I dreamed, all I could see;
Set me on a voyage, a trip unknown,
Till our paths met, and the seeds were sown.
Our journeys became one, our lives we share,
With time we've grown closer, full of love and care.
After thirty-six years that we've been together,
I realize the journey we've taken to find one another
Was only the beginning, a flight plan from above,
To give us a lifetime of happiness and love.

DAILY THOUGHTS

Be safe, light up your space.
Don't participate in an unwanted race.
It's easy to drift where you don't want to be.
However, the experience will help you to see

Let your mind wander.
Set your heart free.
Keep yourself healthy.
With God's wisdom you can see.

It's so gratifying to know someone as true,
To share a few thoughts and learn more about you.
But really there's no need to look very far.
It only takes a glance to see who you are.

If all the world would just try and look,
To see what lies beyond the cover of the book,
As attractive as you are, they soon would see,
Beyond the flesh lies your true beauty.

True friends, special bonds,
They are precious things, forever and a day.
When we fail to nurture them, they begin to fade away.

I write this note on this last day.
Wondering "what's new" that I can say.
You perform your chores, more than your pay,
For those around you along the way,
For all those you make happy or gay,
They see you as a warm sunny ray.

The blessings we feel on a clear sunny day.
Yet we feel so broken when clouds come our way.
Those who are victorious to Him will belong.
No pain, death, or sorrow as they sing a new song.

God places those on your heart, whether family or
        friend,
Their lives are all tangled, no time can they lend.
Don't be discouraged if they seem to not care,
In their silence, they know you are there.

I sit here under the sun;
I wonder what's left to be done?
What I have is what He gave me,
As the dark fades; I start to see,
So under the sun, I soak up its rays.
Not to worry, they're all His days.

I look to the east, no sun I see.
So now it's gone; set itself free.
My chest tightens, anxiety sets in,
For fear, I'll never see it again.
I say to myself, "Why do you care?"
If I don't see, doesn't mean it's not there.
The same with my Lord, He will always care,
Although I can't see Him I know He is there.

If others could see beyond their desire,
You could see what they really require.
Nothing is quite like the way a flower is dressed.
Their content and joy, so freely expressed.
Wrapped in God's garments, pleasing to the eye,
Secure in their faith, need never to cry.
I ponder their existence, wishing mine was the same,
Knowing-
If my life is in turmoil, only I'm to blame.

Steve was born in Pikeville, KY. In 1951, his family moved to North Madison Ohio until they returned to Northern KY in 1957. After finishing school in Bracken County and four years in the Marine Corps, he married Karen Hollar of Bourbon County. It was after his marriage that he started writing poetry. It wasn't a serious hobby at first so regretfully not every poem survived. Still living in Bourbon County, he continues to write poems of encouragement to those around him when he feels the need.

Printed in the United States
By Bookmasters